THE TRICKY TR
AND
THE BILLY GOATS GRUFF

Retold by Cynthia Rider

Illustrated by Melanie Williamson

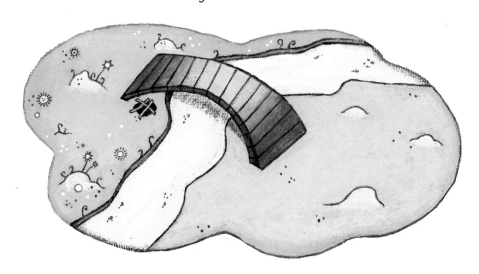

CAMBRIDGE
UNIVERSITY PRESS

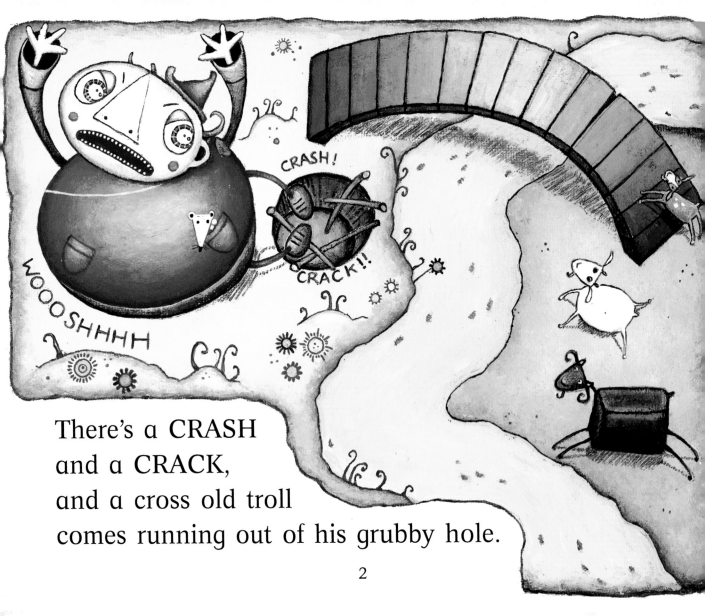

There's a CRASH
and a CRACK,
and a cross old troll
comes running out of his grubby hole.

2

Up on the bridge
going *trit-trit-trot*,
is a little billy goat,
and the troll shouts,
"STOP!"

3

Little billy goat Gruff says,
"Please, let me pass.
Please let me get to the fresh green grass."

4

But the troll is as tricky
as a troll can be.
He says,
"*Nobody* can cross this bridge – but *ME*!"

5

"I shall eat you for dinner,"
he says, with a grin.
"Shall I grill you,
or fry you,
or bake you in a tin?"

6

HEE HEE!

"No, no!" says the goat.
"Please don't eat *me*.
Here comes my brother.
He's fatter than me."

Then onto the bridge,
with a *trit-trit-trot*,
comes the middle billy goat,
and the troll shouts,
"STOP!"

Middle billy goat Gruff says,
"Please, let me pass.
Please let me get to the fresh green grass."

But the troll is as tricky
as a troll can be.
He says,
"*Nobody* can cross this bridge – but *ME*!"

10

"I shall eat you for dinner,"
he says with a grin.
"Shall I grill you,
or fry you,
or bake you in a tin?"

11

"No, no!" says the goat.
"Please, don't eat *me*.
Here comes my brother.
He's fatter than me."

12

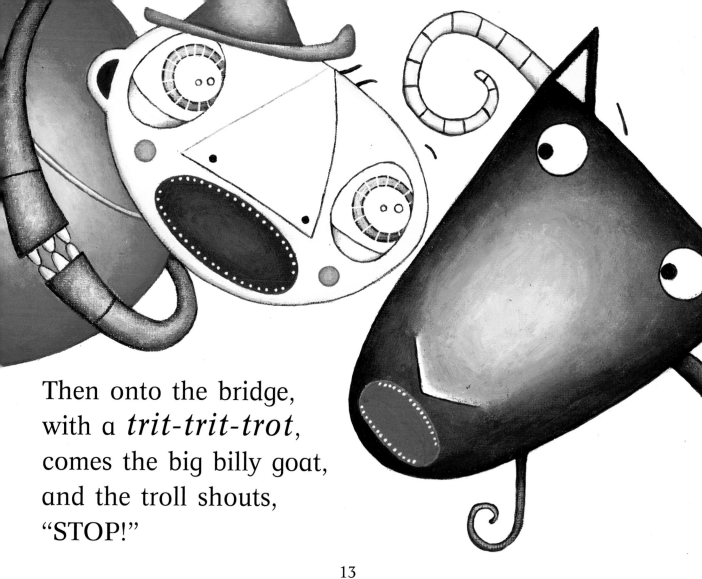

Then onto the bridge,
with a *trit-trit-trot*,
comes the big billy goat,
and the troll shouts,
"STOP!"

The big billy goat goes
CRACK! CRACK! CRASH!
Then down in the river
there's a great big SPLASH!

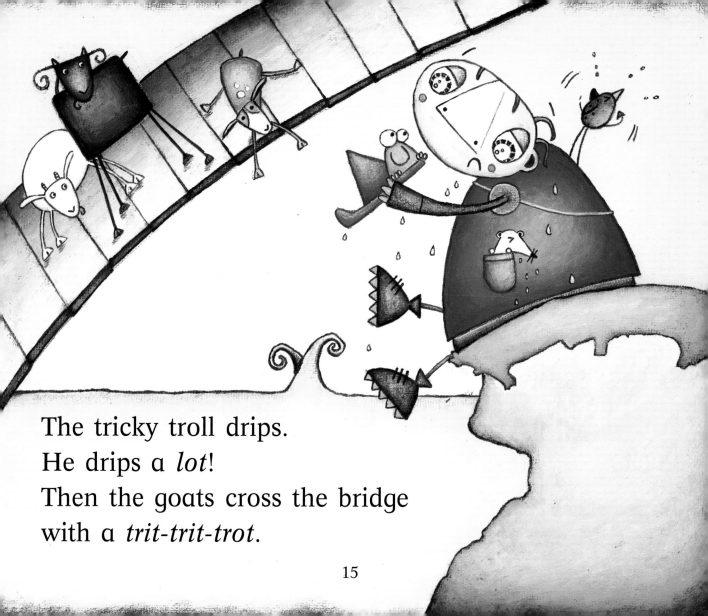

The tricky troll drips.
He drips a *lot*!
Then the goats cross the bridge
with a *trit-trit-trot*.

15

That grass is so green.
That grass is so munchy.
That grass is so fresh
and crisp and crunchy!

16